This book belongs to:

....

Published in 2022 by Welbeck Editions
An imprint of Welbeck Children's Limited,
part of Welbeck Publishing Group.
Based in London and Sydney.
www.welbeckpublishing.com

Text and Illustrations © Welbeck Children's Limited,
part of Welbeck Publishing Group 2022

Art Editor: Deborah Vickers
Designer: Dani Lurie
Associate Publisher: Laura Knowles
Editor: Jenni Lazell

978-1-91351-991-9

Printed in Heshan, China

10 9 8 7 6 5 4 3 2

FSC
www.fsc.org
MIX
Paper | Supporting
responsible forestry
FSC® C020056

AROUND THE WORLD IN 80 MUSICAL INSTRUMENTS

Written by
Nancy Dickmann

Illustrated by
Sue Downing

WELBECK
EDITIONS

Contents

A world of instruments

The world is a big place, full of many countries and cultures. We may wear different clothes, eat different foods, and speak different languages, but there is one thing we all have in common— we all make music.

Making music

If you've ever been to a rock concert, seen a samba band at a carnival, or passed a folk musician busking, then you'll know how powerful and exciting music can be. How many musical instruments can you think of? A lot of people might suggest the guitar, drums, piano, or violin. But there are hundreds more, found all over the world. Each culture has developed its own musical instruments and has used them in different ways. They are played at religious ceremonies and celebrations, alongside dancers, and in concerts.

Finding an instrument

There are sometimes stories on the news about an antique violin being sold for millions of dollars. It's true that a few instruments are very, very expensive, but most of them aren't. In fact, almost anything can be a musical instrument—from an upturned bucket used as a drum to a pair of spoons clicked together in rhythm. Singers, beatboxers, and dancers are proof that even the human body can be a musical instrument!

Types of instruments

Animals are divided into groups such as reptiles, mammals, and birds. In the same way, people who study music try to put musical instruments into groups. There are several different systems, but most are based on how an instrument makes its sound. There are some instruments that you blow into, and others with strings that you pluck, strum, or bow. There are hundreds more instruments that you hit, shake, or scrape. And there are some that don't seem to fit into any category at all!

Pack your bags

It's time to discover some of the huge range of musical instruments found around the world. Some of them are linked to a particular area, while others have spread to many regions, sometimes being adapted and changed when they land somewhere new. Are you ready to begin the journey? Then let's go!

Percussion instruments

Have you ever run a stick along the bars of a metal railing, or tapped with your hands on an upturned bucket? If so, then you've made your own percussion instrument! "Percussion" comes from a Latin word that means to beat or strike. A percussion instrument is one that you hit, scrape, or shake.

Making music

Some of the oldest and simplest instruments that humans have invented are percussion instruments. When you hit, scrape, or shake them, they vibrate and make a sound. Sometimes the vibration is easy to see, such as when the head of a big bass drum is hit. Other vibrations are harder to see, but you can sometimes feel the vibrations in your hands, and you can hear them as well!

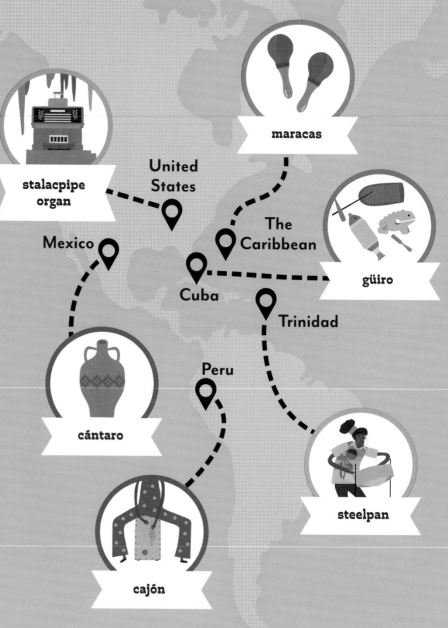

stalacpipe organ

United States

maracas

The Caribbean

güiro

Mexico

Cuba

Trinidad

cántaro

Peru

steelpan

cajón

Around the world

Because many percussion instruments are so simple, they have developed in many different places. People often used whatever materials they could find in the local environment to make their instruments—anything from wood and metal to bones, shells, dried gourds, and animal skins. The instruments are often decorated, so they are beautiful to look at as well as to listen to.

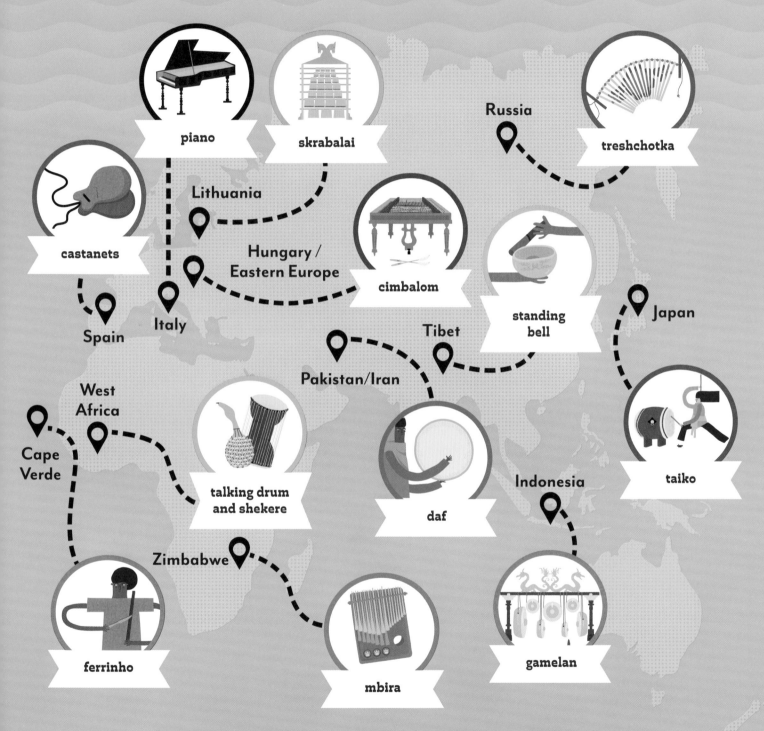

piano

skrabalai

Russia

treshchotka

castanets

Lithuania

Hungary /
Eastern Europe

cimbalom

standing
bell

Japan

Spain

Italy

Tibet

Pakistan/Iran

West
Africa

Cape
Verde

talking drum
and shekere

daf

Indonesia

taiko

Zimbabwe

ferrinho

mbira

gamelan

Percussion instruments play an important role in folk music and dancing in many different cultures. They can also feature in religious ceremonies or be used to inspire soldiers. It's time to learn about some of the varied percussion instruments found around the world!

1. Cajón

A cajón player has to sit on their instrument to play it! This box-like instrument was introduced to Peru by African slaves. A player uses her hands or fingers—or sometimes brushes or mallets—to tap out a rhythm. The hollow box amplifies the sound, and some cajóns have cords stretched across the inside to give a buzzing sound, like a snare drum.

2. Maracas

A rattle is such a simple instrument that even a baby can shake one! Maracas are a type of rattle from South America, and they were originally made from dried gourds filled with seeds or pebbles. They started off as religious instruments but are now used in jazz and Latin music, for which they are played by skilled musicians.

3. Mbira

It would be hard to play a piano using mainly your thumbs. But the mbira, often known as a thumb piano, is designed for that! This instrument comes from Africa and its "keys" are strips of metal or bamboo that a player plucks. The strips are attached in one or two rows to a wooden board, and each one is a different length, so it plays a different note. Mbiras with metal keys first appeared in Zimbabwe and have spread all over Africa. These instruments are often made from recycled materials such as spoon handles or bicycle spokes.

4. Monkey stick

This odd instrument is made of a stout stick or broom handle with metal "jingles" fastened onto it. Metal beer-bottle tops are often used, which is why the monkey stick is called a "lagerphone" in Australia. It was probably inspired by a similar stick with bells used by British military bands. To play a monkey stick, you shake it or bang it on the ground to make the jingles rattle. Some versions have a boot at the bottom for this purpose!

5. Stalacpipe organ

Imagine being inside a musical cave! Would you find it funny or spooky? In the 1950s, Leland Sprinkle built the Great Stalacpipe Organ in a cave in Virginia. He attached rubber mallets to different stalactites throughout the cave. Each one makes a different note as it hits the stalactite. The mallets are controlled by a console like an organ.

6. Piano

Sometimes you want to play music quietly, and at other times you want to make some noise! The musician who invented the piano in the early 1700s wanted to be able to control the volume when he played. Pressing a piano key makes a hammer inside the instrument strike a string. The harder you press, the louder the sound! Because the strings are hit rather than plucked or bowed, a piano is often grouped with the percussion instruments. It is one of most versatile instruments around, used in everything from classical music to jazz and rock and roll.

11

7.Steelpan

The sun is shining, the weather is warm, and there's a smell of the ocean in the air. It's the ideal Caribbean scene, made even more perfect by the jangly sound of a steel band playing.

These musicians are playing instruments called steelpans. They are sometimes known instead as steel drums, but technically they not drums at all—they are a type of gong. Traditionally, these instruments are made from the bottoms of large steel oil barrels. The surface is hammered inward to form areas of different shapes—a bit like the shapes on a soccer ball. Hitting each area with a rubber mallet gives a different pitch, so a single steelpan can play a melody.

Steelpans were invented on the island of Trinidad, where
poor musicians used whatever they could find to make their
instruments. Some early versions were made from buckets
and cans! Musicians playing steelpans performed during the
Carnival celebrations each year, with rival neighborhoods
competing to see who could produce the best music. Soon
this new instrument and musical style spread throughout the
Caribbean. There are different types of steelpans in a steel
band. Some play the melody, while lower-pitched pans sound
out the rhythm and harmony.

8. Gong

A gong is a flat metal disk that you hit with a mallet. Gongs can be hung from a frame or can sit on a cushion. They are famous for loud crashing noises, but some gongs make a delicate chiming sound instead. They are common in Asia, where gongs of different pitches can form an orchestra.

9. Standing bell

These bells rest upside down, rather than being hung. Striking them with a mallet makes a peaceful, sustained sound. If you rub the rim with a mallet, it plays a long note that sounds like singing. It is perfect for accompanying meditation in the Buddhist areas of China, such as Tibet, where these bowls are used.

10. Skrabalai

Many bells make up the skrabalai, from Lithuania. The wooden bells are arranged in rows on a frame, and each one rings a different pitch. A musician plays a tune by hitting one bell after another with two wooden sticks.

11. Castanets

It's very hard to dance and play an instrument at the same time, but castanet players make it look easy! Castanets are a pair of hollowed-out pieces of wood, held together by a cord—they look like a clamshell. Dancers in Spain open and close them to clap out a rhythm as they dance.

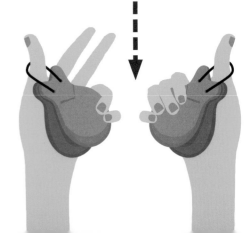

14

12. Treshchotka

With the Russian treshchotka, you can create your own applause! It has up to 20 thin wooden boards threaded together on a rope. The player holds one end of the rope in each hand and moves it back and forth. This makes the boards hit each other to produce a sound like hands clapping.

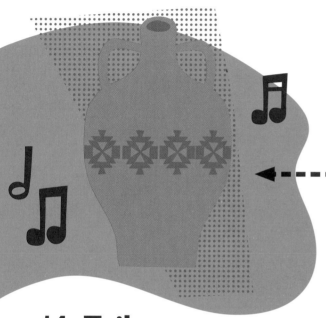

13. Cántaro

Have you ever played a tune on your dishes? The cántaro is a clay pot used to make music. Hitting the outside or the mouth of the pot with your hand makes a range of different sounds. And putting water in the pot changes the pitch! It is an important instrument in Mexican folk music.

14. Taiko

Taiko are barrel-shaped Japanese drums. Smaller versions have a head about the size of a dinner plate, while the largest ones may be six feet wide! Long ago, they were used to inspire soldiers and in traditional Japanese theater. Today, groups of skilled drummers thrill audiences with their performances.

15. Talking drum

Can a drum report the news? The West African talking drum can! A player holds the drum between his arm and his body. When he squeezes, it pulls on the cords surrounding the drum, changing the pitch. A skilled drummer can produce a sound very similar to a person talking. They have been used to send messages from one village to another.

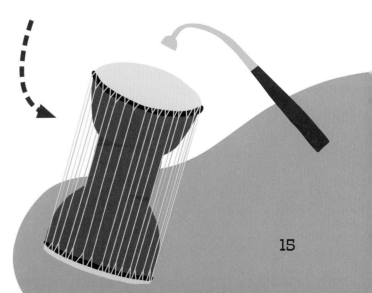

Drums around the world

There are so many types of drums found all over the world that you could easily fill this book with drums alone! Musicians play them solo, in drum ensembles, or as part of a band or orchestra that includes many different instruments.

Types of drums

Have you ever seen a drummer using a drum set in pop or rock videos? They play several different drums at once, including snare drum, bass drum, and toms. Tall conga drums, from Cuba, are also played in sets, in which each drum plays a different pitch.

Congas are a type of hand drum—you don't need drumsticks to play them. Bongos and tablas are also hand drums, and so is the African djembe drum. This goblet-shaped drum makes a powerful sound. A drummer can produce different pitches by hitting different areas of the drumhead.

Frame drums have a simple ring-shaped frame covered with a skin. You use your fingers to tap some frame drums, such as the Persian daf. Others, like the Irish bodhrán, are played with a stick.

Parts of a drum

Drums come in all shapes and sizes, but their essential form is the same: a thin membrane stretched tight over a rigid shell. The shell is often shaped like a cylinder or a bowl, and it can be made of wood, metal, or plastic. For thousands of years, the membrane (called the drumhead) was made of animal skin. That's why people sometimes talk about "playing the skins"! Today they are often made from plastic instead.

When you hit a drum, either with your hand or with a drumstick, the drumhead vibrates and makes a sound. Drumheads are held in place with nails or rings or are lashed with cords. The tighter they are stretched, the higher the sound the drum will make.

Using drums

Can you imagine music without drums? It would certainly be very different! Drums provide the beat for musical groups, and the way they are played sets the mood. A drumbeat can be slow and chilled, fast and furious, or somewhere in between.

Drums play a part in all kinds of music, from rock and pop to samba, jazz, folk music, and even orchestral pieces. They also sound wonderful on their own. All-drum groups produce pulse-pounding rhythms—and make a very impressive noise!

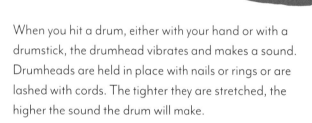

17

16. Shekere

Take one large gourd, some thread, and a bunch of beads or shells, and you can make a musical instrument! The shekere, from West Africa, is a large gourd that has been dried and hollowed out. A woven net of beads or shells surrounds it, and when a musician shakes or taps the gourd, the net hits it, sounding out a rhythm. There are similar instruments in other parts of Africa and the Caribbean.

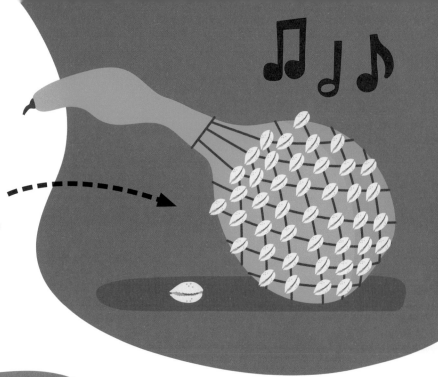

17. Daf

A drum called a daf has been played in Persia (now Iran) for thousands of years. It's made of a skin stretched tight over a round wooden frame. Musicians hold the frame with their thumbs or palms and use their fingers to tap out a rhythm. On the inside of the frame are metal rings that jingle when the drum is played, and musicians shake the daf to get more sound from the metal rings. The sound of the daf often accompanies religious ceremonies.

18. Jaw harp

Many instruments have a hollow chamber to allow the sound to resonate. With a jaw harp, the player's own mouth is the chamber! The harp's flexible metal tongue is attached to a stiff frame. A player holds the frame against her teeth and plucks the harp's tongue. It creates a twangy sound that is sometimes heard in country music, as well as in many other genres around the world.

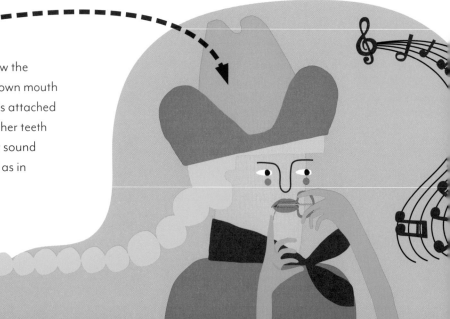

19. Cimbalom

A cimbalom looks a little like a piano that's been laid on its side and opened up to reveal the metal strings. To play it, you use a pair of wooden mallets to hit the strings—about 125 of them! This instrument has a bright, metallic sound and is played across eastern Europe, particularly in the music of the Jewish and Roma people.

20. Ferrinho

The island nation of Cape Verde, off the African coast, is the home of the ferrinho. This simple instrument is a long metal bar that a player holds in one hand, with the other end resting on his shoulder. He scrapes up and down with a smaller metal bar to create a rhythm. A ferrinho often pairs with an accordion to play a style of music called *funaná*.

21. Güiro

This Cuban instrument is usually made from wood or a dried gourd. A player uses a stick to scrape along the ridges carved into one side, creating a rasping sound. In the Dominican Republic, musicians use a stiff brush to play the güira—a similar instrument that is made of metal and looks a bit like a cheese grater.

Music and war

Some kinds of music can relax you. Others make you want to get up and dance! But throughout history, music has been used for another purpose too: to inspire soldiers in battle.

Long, long ago

The Bible tells the story of Joshua, a military leader who wanted to capture the walled city of Jericho. His army had trumpets made from rams' horns. Joshua ordered them all to be blown at once, and the sound made Jericho's walls crumble! The story is probably not true, but it shows that people believed in the power of music.

Helping soldiers

The ancient Greeks and Romans—as well as many other cultures—used drums to help keep their soldiers in step, both in training and on the battlefield. They also used trumpets, such as the huge, curving Roman buccina. Trumpets were especially useful because their clear, piercing tones could be heard over the noise of the fighting. Commanders used them to send messages and give orders in the heat of a battle. Different melodies told soldiers to march, retreat, attack, and more. The sound of music could also give tired soldiers a morale boost.

Frightening the enemy

Music could also be used to intimidate the enemy. During the Crusades (1095–1291), European armies came face to face with the highly trained military bands of the Saracens. These bands, armed only with drums and trumpets, gave motivation and orders for their own army, and their impressive sound frightened the attackers—especially their horses.

In the 1700s, the people of Scotland rose up against the English king, and their armies were accompanied on the field by the wailing skirl of bagpipes. Scottish regiments in the British army continued to be piped into battle, a practice that went on into the twentieth century.

Music as a weapon

In recent years, music has been used as a weapon. Armies have brought in huge speakers and played aggressive music very loudly to make an enemy give in. Sometimes people were forced to listen to loud heavy metal—or annoying pop songs—for days on end. That's definitely not what the musicians had in mind when they recorded their songs!

22. Gamelan ------->

The gamelan isn't a single instrument. In fact, it's a whole percussion orchestra! The gamelan comes from the Indonesian islands of Java and Bali, and each island has its own distinct style. A typical gamelan includes gongs, drums, xylophones, and metal bars that are struck with mallets. They often also include nonpercussion instruments such as flutes or a type of stringed instrument called a rebab. The sound of a gamelan is often accompanied by one or more singers to provide a melody. You might hear them at Indonesian weddings, concerts, dance performances, or shadow-puppet theater.

23. Xylophone

When you hit a wooden bar with a mallet, the pitch that it makes depends on its size and shape. A xylophone is made up of many different bars, each playing a different pitch. Musicians play them with mallets that often have rubber tips. Different types of xylophones are found around the world. The marimba, often used in Latin America, has a vertical tube below each bar. These tubes are often made of metal, and they help the sound resonate. In the West African balafon, dried gourds of different sizes are used in place of the tubes.

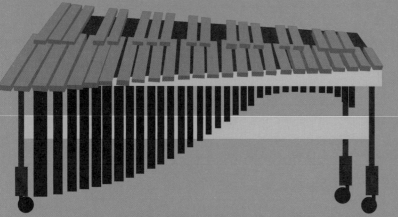

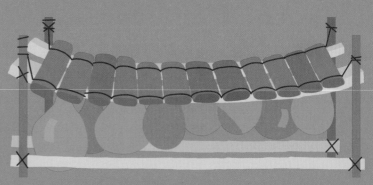

MAKE YOUR OWN

It's time to make your own percussion instrument! The agogo is an instrument made up of two bells that originally came from West Africa. From there, it spread to the Americas, and it is now a familiar sound in the samba bands that perform at Carnival in Brazil. Each of the bells in an agogo plays a different pitch.

What you need:

- Two empty, round containers of different sizes with metal bottoms
- Strong, wide rubber bands or duct tape
- A wooden spoon (or anything else that can be used as a drumstick)
- Paint, markers, and stickers to decorate

What to do:

1 Remove the lids and check the sounds that your containers make when you hit the metal bottom. Choose two that make different sounds—one higher and one lower.

2 Place the containers next to each other with the metal bottoms pointing in the same direction, but with one higher than the other.

3 Stick them firmly together with rubber bands or duct tape.

4 Decorate your agogo however you like!

5 Experiment with different rhythms, tapping the "bells" of your agogo with your drumstick. You can find videos online to inspire you.

stringed instruments

Have you ever watched a video of a famous violinist or an electric guitar maestro and been blown away by their skill? It might make you think that these types of instruments are too hard for you to play. But violins and guitars are just two members of the stringed instrument family, and if you've ever twanged a rubber band, then you've played one too!

Making music

A stringed instrument has at least one string—the clue is in the name. Long ago, many strings were made from animal hair or intestines, but today they are often made of metal or plastic instead. When the string vibrates, it makes a sound, and making the string shorter (such as by pressing down on a guitar string) makes the pitch higher. Most stringed instruments have a hollow body to amplify the vibrations.

Earth harp, Appalachian dulcimer

United States

Mexico

guitarrón

Hawaii

ukulele

Bolivia

Chile

guitarrón chileno

charango

Around the world

You'll find stringed instruments in all corners of the world. In many places, they were made from whatever materials were available. Wooden bodies are very common, but some have been made using dried gourds or tortoise shells—and even armadillo shells! The instruments are often decorated with inlays of shells, wood, or mother-of-pearl.

Celtic harp

violin and cello

jouhikko

Russia

balalaika

Finland

bouzouki

tanbur

koto

British Isles

Italy

Greece

Turkey

Iran

China

Japan

India

West Africa

Niger

Ethiopia

Vietnam

erhu

begena

kora

Botswana

sitar

k'ni

imzad

mouth bow

oud

Stringed instruments are incredibly versatile. From a cello soloist playing a classical piece to a fiddler scraping out a jig or an electric guitarist shredding, these instruments can play all kinds of music. Are you ready to discover some of the strings used around the world?

24. Violin - - - - - - - - - - - ->

The violin is one of the best-known stringed instruments. It is fairly small, with four strings that a musician plays with a bow to produce a singing tone. The violin as we know it today evolved in Italy in the 1500s, but it was based on earlier stringed instruments. It is a familiar sight in classical music, but it also has a secret identity: the "fiddle" used in folk and country music is actually just another name for a violin.

<- - - - - - - - - 25. Erhu

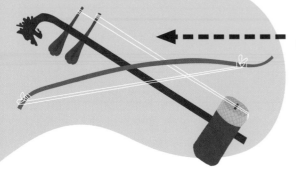

The Chinese erhu is sometimes called a "vertical fiddle." Unlike a violin, which a musician holds between her chin and shoulder, the body of an erhu rests on the player's lap. It is a small box, covered on one side with snakeskin that vibrates when it's played. An erhu has a long neck and two strings, and it is played with a bow.

To bow or not to bow

With some instruments, a musician pulls a bow across the strings to make them vibrate. The bow is usually made of horsehair and rubbed with a substance called rosin, which helps the bow grip and pull on the strings. Other stringed instruments are plucked or strummed instead. Plucking with your fingertips makes a soft, mellow sound, while using fingernails or a plastic plectrum (pick) makes a harder, brighter sound.

26. Cello

It might be tempting to call the cello an oversized violin, but it's much more than that! The two instruments are closely related, though a cello plays lower notes and is big enough that you have to sit down to play it. Its rich, mellow sound—and the range of notes that it plays—make it close in sound to the human voice.

27. Imzad

Among the Tuareg people of the Sahara, the imzad plays a special role. This instrument is made from a dried gourd cut in half, with the open side covered with an animal skin. It has a single string and is played with a bow to accompany poems and songs about heroes of the past. What makes the imzad unique is that it is played only by women.

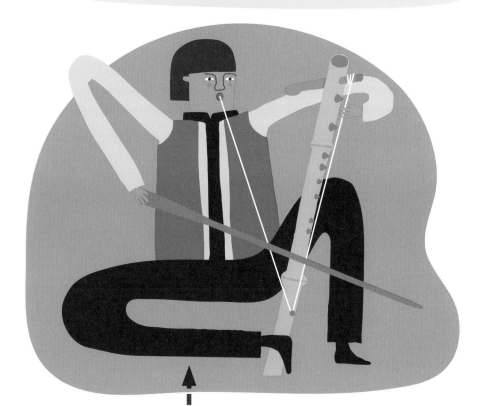

28. Jouhikko

Finland is a long way from Greece, but it is the home of the jouhikko, which is a descendant of the lyres played by the ancient Greeks. A jouhikko has three strings attached to a wooden frame, and it is played with a bow. One string plays a constant note while the others play a melody over the top. A similar instrument called the talharpa is played in neighboring Estonia.

29. K'ni

The k'ni sounds even more like singing than a cello does. That's because it has no hollow chamber—instead, the player's mouth does that job! A k'ni is a bamboo stick with a single string and a bamboo bow. A player holds a string—which is attached to the string of the k'ni—in his mouth. By changing the shape of his mouth, he can change the sound.

The Earth harp is made up of strings attached to a wide bridge. There are also hollow chambers to amplify the sound. The harp can be installed in a concert hall or outdoors, with the chambers and bridge on the stage. The strings stretch out over the audience, and their far ends can be attached to the back wall of the concert arena or to a nearby tower or skyscraper—or even the top of a mountain! In one setup, the Earth harp's strings were 957.05 feet long, giving it the world record as the longest playable stringed instrument.

30. Earth harp

Can you imagine going to a concert where you sit inside the instrument being played? This is what happens to people who watch William Close perform on the Earth harp he invented.

Playing such a large instrument isn't easy! The musician stands just in front of the bridge, in the middle of the strings. Wearing gloves coated in rosin (the same sticky substance that violin players put on their bows), he runs his hands along the strings to produce a sound wave. It's similar to the effect when you rub your finger around the rim of a glass. One listener described the experience as "like being inside a giant cello."

The orchestra

An orchestra is one of the best-known types of musical groups. Orchestras began in Europe, but they are now found all over the world. Some people might think that orchestras only play old-fashioned classical music, but in fact an orchestra can play almost anything, from movie scores to pop music!

Sections of the orchestra

Most orchestras have the same instruments, arranged into four sections. They are stringed, brass, woodwind, and percussion. Other instruments, such as a piano, organ, or guitar, sometimes join an orchestra for a featured solo. More than half of the musicians in an orchestra play stringed instruments. A large orchestra might have more than 30 violins! Stringed instruments are not as loud as woodwinds and brass, so you need a lot more players for them to be heard over the other instruments.

The conductor

With so many musicians, keeping them playing together is a big job. The orchestra's conductor stands at the front, sometimes on a raised platform. They have a copy of the music that shows the parts for all the instruments. With their right hand, the conductor marks the beat. Their left hand is used to give signals to different sections, such as telling them to start playing, get louder, or come to a dramatic stop.

Big or small?

A full-size orchestra often has about 100 musicians, but there are smaller groups too. A chamber orchestra has no more than 50, so they can play in smaller rooms and concert halls. Musicians sometimes play in even smaller groups, such as a string quartet, which has two violins, a viola, and a cello.

Thinking outside the box

Musical works written for orchestras sometimes include some pretty unusual instruments. Some use percussion instruments like sleigh bells to give a Christmassy feel. In "The Typewriter"—a piece by Leroy Anderson—one soloist sits at a table and plays a typewriter! Its clickety-clack sound forms part of the music. The Russian composer Pyotr Tchaikovsky wrote his 1812 Overture to celebrate a Russian victory in a famous battle. At one point, cannons go off!

31. Celtic harp

This harp has been played in Ireland and Scotland for at least a thousand years. The frame has a large, hollow soundbox carved from a single log, and is strung with metal strings. It was played at feasts and celebrations, accompanying songs or poems. The harp was such an important part of Gaelic culture that it appears on coins and coats of arms.

32. Begena

The Ethiopian begena is an instrument with an even longer history. According to legend, it is the harp played by King David in the Bible! A begena has ten strings, and they have pieces of leather attached that make a buzzing sound when the string is plucked. The instrument is mainly used for praying and religious ceremonies.

33. Koto

On the Japanese koto, strings are stretched across a curved wooden base that is as long as an adult is tall. The strings are traditionally made of silk, and a musician wears fingerpicks to pluck them. The koto is a very traditional instrument, but some modern musicians are bringing it up to date by using it to play jazz and pop music.

34. Appalachian dulcimer

The Appalachian dulcimer is a key part of the folk music from this North American mountain region. A player strums the three or four strings with one hand while the other hand presses down on the strings to change pitch. There is a special version of the instrument that two people can play. They sit facing each other with the dulcimer across their knees, and each person has a set of strings to play.

35. Ukulele

Would you want to play an instrument called the "jumping flea"? That's what "ukulele" means in the Hawaiian language, but luckily this instrument doesn't bite! It looks like a small, four-stringed guitar. Ukuleles are used in traditional Hawaiian music as well as jazz, pop, and reggae. They are cheap to make and easy to play, which has made them very popular.

36. Guitarrón

You have to be strong to play the guitarrón! This large, heavy instrument is famous as part of Mexican mariachi bands. Its size gives it a loud, deep sound—perfect for playing the bass line in mariachi music. It takes a lot of finger strength to press down and pluck the thick, heavy strings.

37. Charango

At the other end of the scale, the charango—played in the Andes of South America—is tiny. It is similar in size and shape to a ukulele, but it has ten strings while a ukulele has only four. The body of a charango is traditionally made from the shell of an armadillo!

38. Guitarrón chileno

A standard guitar has six strings, but its cousin from Chile has 25. This tricky instrument is played by poets who use it to accompany their songs. Four of the strings are shorter and attached to the instrument's body, rather than its neck. They are called "diabilitos," meaning "little devils," and they make a high-pitched sound.

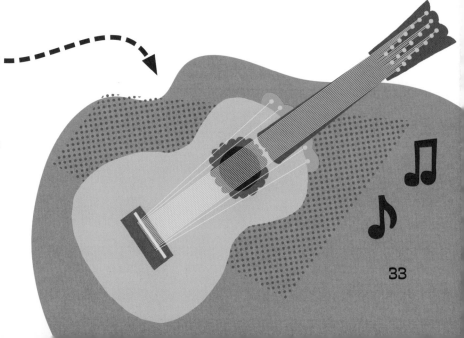

33

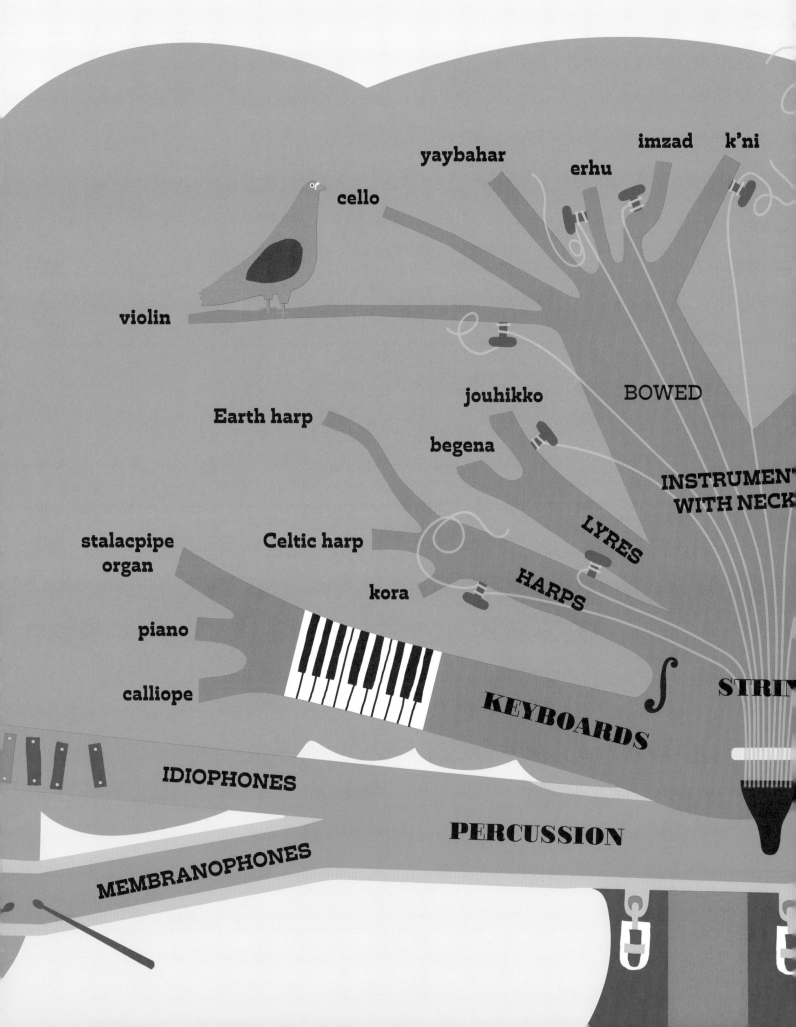

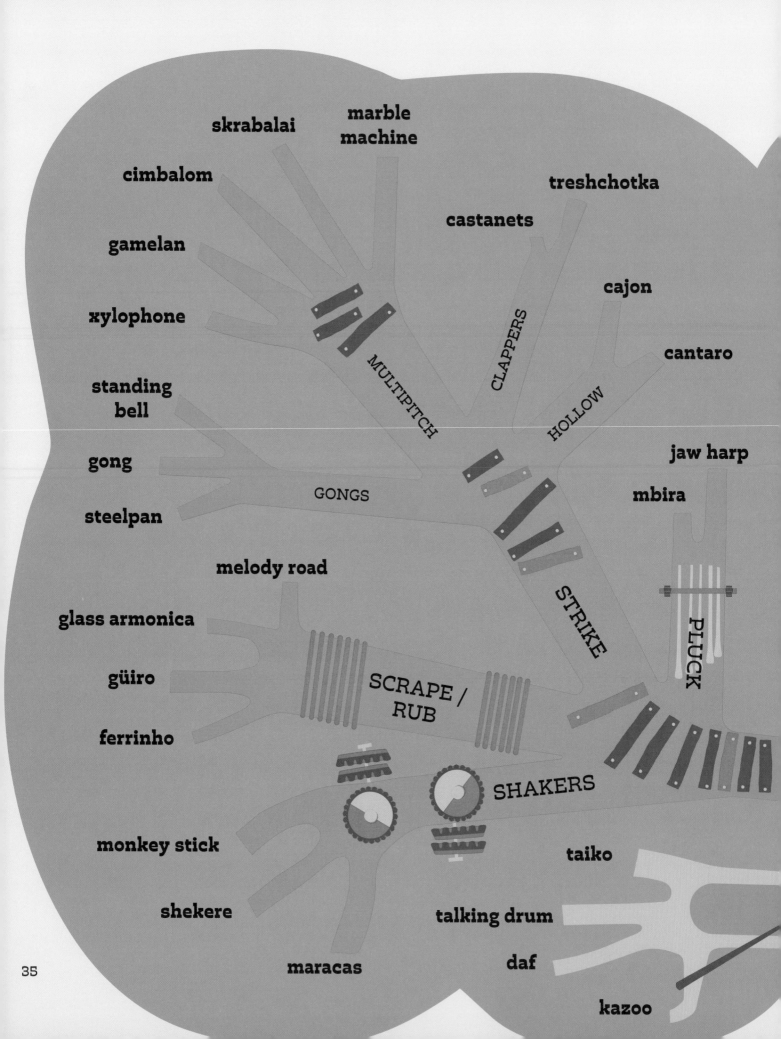

skrabalai

marble machine

cimbalom

treshchotka

gamelan

castanets

xylophone

cajon

standing bell

cantaro

CLAPPERS

MULTIPITCH

HOLLOW

jaw harp

gong

mbira

GONGS

steelpan

melody road

STRIKE

glass armonica

PLUCK

güiro

SCRAPE / RUB

ferrinho

SHAKERS

monkey stick

taiko

shekere

talking drum

maracas

daf

kazoo

A musical family tree

What a lot of instruments there are! Some of them, like the cello and guitar, have a lot in common. But others, like the maracas and the theremin, couldn't be more different. How can we make sense of them all?

Scientists try to put animals in order by grouping them into families, such as mammals and reptiles. The members of each family have a lot in common—for example, mammals are all warm-blooded animals that produce milk to feed their babies. The group is then divided into smaller branches, such as cats, apes, rodents, and bears. In this way, you can make a family tree of the animal world. (In case you're wondering, you belong to the ape branch . . .)

We can do the same thing with musical instruments! There are lots of different ways that you can group them. You might separate them by whether they make a high sound, a low sound, or a sound somewhere in between. You could organize them by the culture or country that they come from. You could even group them based on how they are used—for example, for religious purposes or sending signals.

In this book, we've grouped instruments based on how they make their sound. This means that drums form a single family, even though they come in a huge range of sizes and styles. It's not a perfect system—some instruments might fit into more than one group, and some of the modern experimental instruments are hard to classify at all! Turn the page to see how the instruments in this book are related.

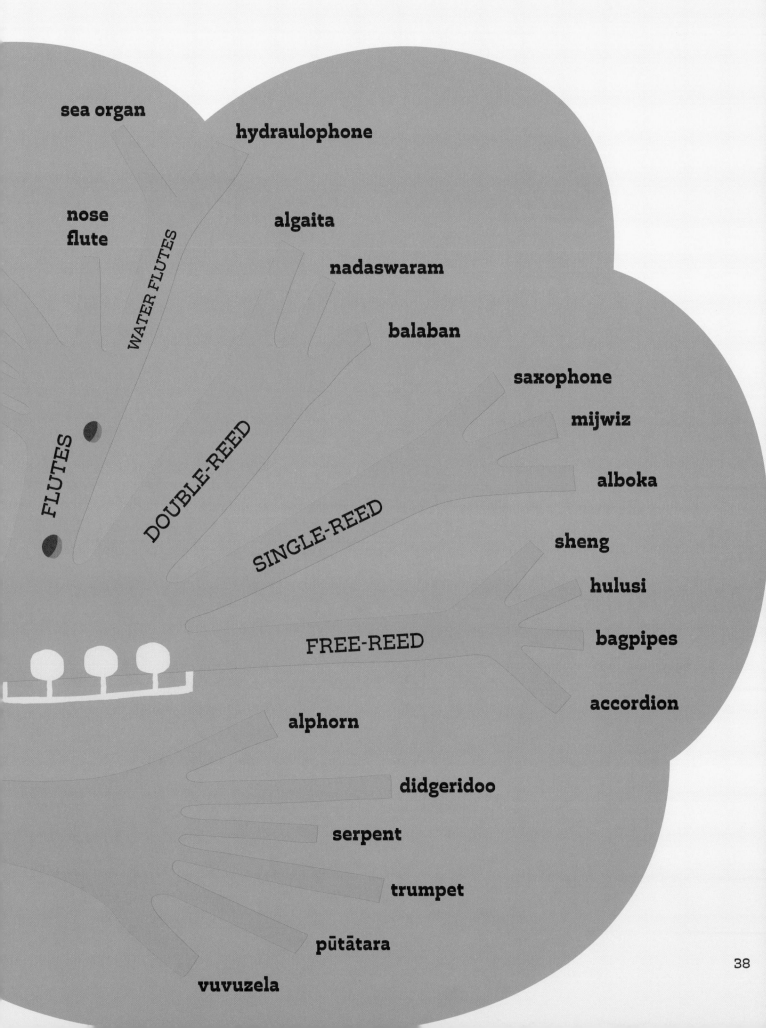

sea organ

hydraulophone

nose flute

WATER FLUTES

algaita

nadaswaram

balaban

saxophone

mijwiz

alboka

FLUTES

DOUBLE-REED

SINGLE-REED

sheng

hulusi

bagpipes

FREE-REED

accordion

alphorn

didgeridoo

serpent

trumpet

pūtātara

vuvuzela

guitarrón

charango

oud

chileno

guitarron

siku

sitar

tanbur

ukulele

atenteben

bouzouki

dizi

SHORT
NECKS

LONG
NECKS

ocarina

balalaika

PLUCKED

hurdy-gurdy

wheelharp

WITH A WHEEL

koto

Appalachian dulcimer

ZITHERS

mouth-bow

WOODWIND

WIND

BRASS

ELECTRIC
INSTRUMENTS

theremin

Moog synthesiser

Zeusaphone

39. Mouth bow

The mouth bow may look more like a weapon, but it plays music rather than shooting arrows! Musical bows are played in many places around the world, where they often have a hollow gourd to amplify the sound. The mouth bow, which is common in southern Africa, uses the player's mouth instead of a gourd. They hold the bow in their mouth while plucking or bowing the string.

40. Balalaika

It would be hard to mistake the Russian balalaika for anything else. Its unique triangular shape makes it easier to build but hard to hold as you play. The hollow body has a small sound hole and three strings that are strummed or plucked. Balalaikas are played in Russian folk music, and there are also orchestras made up of balalaikas of different sizes.

41. Bouzouki

Like the balalaika, the Greek bouzouki is a type of lute, but it has a round body and four (or sometimes three) pairs of strings. When a player plucks the metal strings with a plectrum, it produces a bright, metallic sound. Bouzoukis are still a very common sight in Greek folk music, and they often accompany dancers.

40

42. Oud

Balalaikas and bouzoukis are old, but their ancestor—the oud—is much, much older. It comes from the Middle East, and its name means "wood" in Arabic. In the early days, the strings of this ancient instrument were plucked with the quill of an eagle's feather. Over the centuries, the oud spread throughout Europe and evolved into many different instruments, but the traditional form is still played across the Arab world.

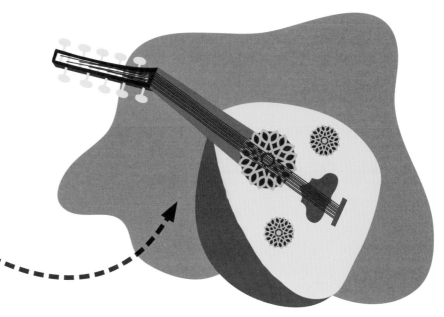

43. Sitar

When it comes to musical instruments, gourds really get around, and a large one forms the body of the Indian sitar. The instrument's long neck has about 20 strings for the player to pluck or strum. Some of them are drone strings, which produce a sustained single note that complements the other notes that the musician plays.

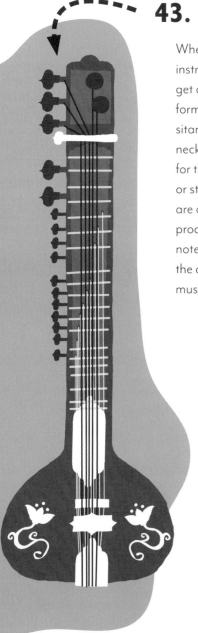

44. Tanbur

The tanbur has a very long neck, but it is much thinner than a sitar's. The tanbur's round body and long neck make it look a bit like a banjo, and the length of the neck gives it a deep sound. Like the oud, this is a very ancient instrument, and today it is played in Turkey and other parts of southwest and central Asia. The version played in Turkey has six strings, arranged in three pairs.

45. Kora

Is it a harp? Is it a lute? No, it's a kora! This instrument from West Africa is a bit of both. Its body is made from half of a large gourd called a calabash. A long, wooden neck goes into the gourd, and it holds the 21 strings. They pass over a bridge that sticks out from the gourd at a right angle to the neck. Each string plays a different note, although they can be adjusted by sliding a leather ring up or down the neck. A musician uses both hands to pluck the strings to play a melody.

46. Hurdy-gurdy

The hurdy-gurdy is another instrument that looks like a mix of other types. It's a little like a violin, but instead of using a bow, the player turns a handle at the end. This spins a wheel with rosin on the rim, which rubs against the strings to make them vibrate. To change notes, there is a keyboard that presses wedges of wood against the strings. Several drone strings play constantly to accompany the melody, like the drone of bagpipes. In fact, "a bagpipe with strings instead of pipes" is a pretty good description of this odd instrument!

MAKE YOUR OWN

In poor communities in the American South, many aspiring young blues musicians learned to play on a simple, homemade instrument called a diddley bow. It has only one string and is sometimes called a "jitterbug" or "one-string." Why not try making your own?

What you need:

- A long, narrow wooden board
- A length of wire
- Two screws and a screwdriver
- An empty glass jar or tin
- Something to use as a slide, such as a nail or a small glass jar to put over your finger

What to do:

1 Screw the screws into the board, one at each end, leaving three-quarters of an inch sticking out. (If you don't have screws, use a hammer and nails—with help from an adult!)

2 Attach one end of the wire to one screw, and the other end to the other screw.

3 Wedge the glass jar or tin on its side between the wire and the board, and tighten the wire until the jar is held firmly in place. The jar will act as a bridge and also amplify the sound.

4 Pluck the string with one hand and use the other to press a slide against the string. This changes the length of the wire—and the pitch too! Experiment to see if you can play a tune. You can find videos online to inspire you.

43

Wind instruments

Have you ever blown into a seashell to make a trumpeting sound or whistled with a blade of grass? If so, then you've played a wind instrument! Members of this large and diverse family can be as simple as a penny whistle or as complicated as a saxophone.

Making music

Wind instruments make a sound when a column of air inside the instrument vibrates. Most types have holes or valves that let the player change the pitch by making the air column longer or shorter. The longer it is, the lower the pitch, which equals a lower sound. Smaller instruments make higher sounds.

kazoo

calliope

ocarina

siku

United States

Central America

Bolivia

Hawaii

nose flute

Wood, brass, and more

Wind instruments are often divided into two families: woodwind and brass. Many of the instruments in these families are made from wood or brass, but others aren't. You'll find wind instruments around the world made from bones, gourds, bamboo, reeds, and even shells. Archaeologists have found simple flutes carved from animal bones that are tens of thousands of years old. Since then, flutes and other wind instruments have evolved all over the world.

44

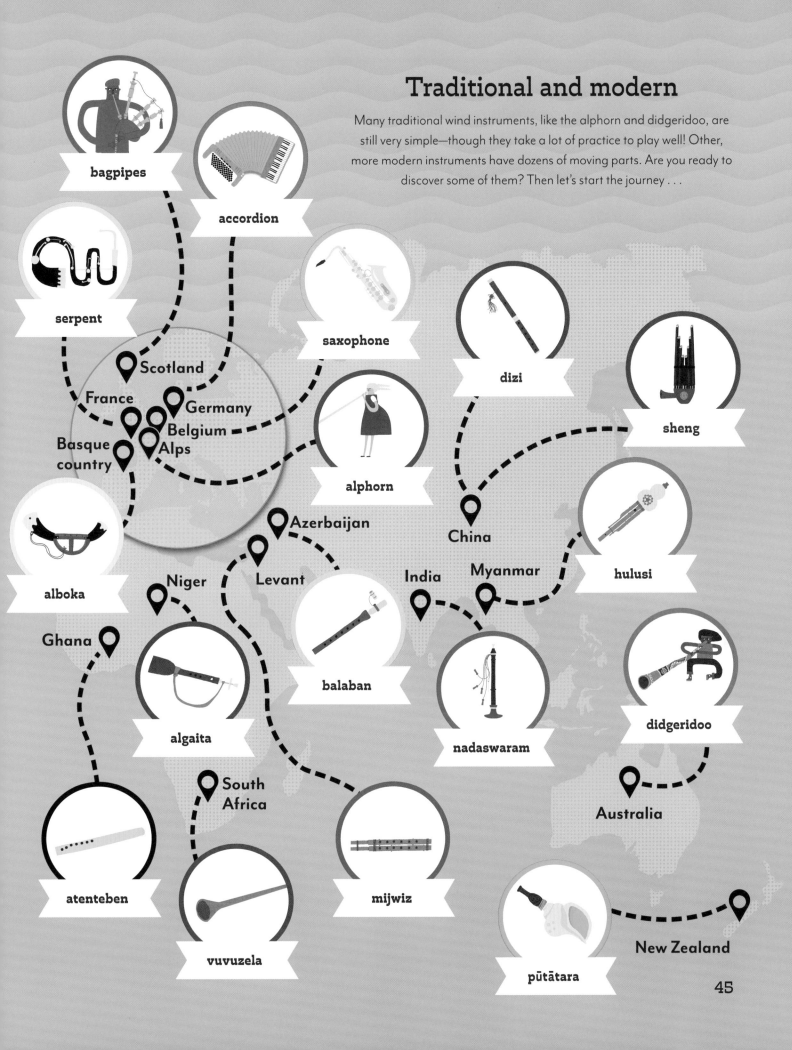

Traditional and modern

Many traditional wind instruments, like the alphorn and didgeridoo, are still very simple—though they take a lot of practice to play well! Other, more modern instruments have dozens of moving parts. Are you ready to discover some of them? Then let's start the journey . . .

bagpipes

accordion

serpent

saxophone

dizi

sheng

Scotland

France

Germany

Belgium

Basque country

Alps

alphorn

hulusi

China

alboka

Azerbaijan

Niger

Levant

India

Myanmar

Ghana

balaban

didgeridoo

algaita

nadaswaram

South Africa

Australia

atenteben

mijwiz

vuvuzela

New Zealand

pūtātara

47. Dizi

You've probably seen the silver flutes played in marching bands and orchestras. But not all flutes look the same—and not all of them are made of metal! The Chinese dizi is made from a piece of hollow bamboo with finger holes drilled into it. A thin membrane, like tissue paper, is glued over the hole that the player blows across. It gives the dizi a unique buzzing sound.

48. Nose flute

With most wind instruments, the musician blows into them using their mouth. But the flutes found in Hawaii and other Pacific islands use the player's nose instead! A musician holds one nostril closed and uses the other to blow into a flute, usually made of bone, bamboo, or wood. Its soft, gentle sound is perfect for love songs. In some places there are double flutes that need both nostrils to play.

49. Siku

People in the Andes Mountains of South America also make flutes from bamboo. These flutes don't have finger holes, so each tube can only play one pitch. Instead, about a dozen tubes of different lengths are tied together in rows. The player blows across the open ends of the tubes, moving from one tube to another to create a melody. Similar instruments—often called panpipes—are found in different cultures around the world.

50. Atenteben

The atenteben is a bamboo flute from Ghana that you play by blowing into one end—a little like a recorder. Most versions have six finger holes along the top and one on the bottom. The sound of the atenteben is heard at ceremonies, such as funeral processions, but musicians use it in jazz and other types of modern music as well.

51. Ocarina

The ocarina is proof that musical instruments can be cool to look at as well as nice to hear. You blow into these hollow ceramic shapes, covering the finger holes to change the pitch. These simple flutes have been used by people around the world for thousands of years. The Maya and Aztecs of Central America and Mexico played ocarinas, and they were often shaped to look like people or animals.

52. Calliope

People are always looking for ways to use new technology to make music, and that's how the calliope was invented! In the 1850s, steam power ruled the world, and one American inventor used it to play a tune! The calliope is like an organ made up of whistles, and a boiler forces steam through the pipes to make them play a tune. Often made using train whistles, calliopes were very loud and could attract a crowd to a circus or fair.

Supersize me

Many instruments are small enough for a musician to hold in their hands. Others are so big that they have to be played sitting down—or sometimes even standing up! As a general rule, the bigger the instrument, the deeper (and bigger) the sound it makes. And some instruments are very large indeed . . .

Instrument families

Many instruments come in different versions—some play high and others play low. For example, the flute that you see in orchestras is just one version of the instrument. There is also an enormous subcontrabass flute, which is taller than its player. There are supersized versions of the clarinet and saxophone too. Someone even built a tuba that was more than 6.5 feet tall!

It's not just wind instruments that can be supersized. There is a huge bass version of the banjo, which a musician has to stand up to play. And remember the triangular Russian balalaika? The most common version is a little smaller than a guitar, but there is a smaller, higher-pitched version called the piccolo balalaika, and several larger ones, including the giant contrabass. It is so large that it has to rest on the ground!

How low can you go?

The violin is the smallest member of another family of instruments. The viola is slightly larger, the cello is even bigger, and the double bass has to be played standing up. But there is a rare instrument called the octobass which is even larger—about 11.5 feet tall! A musician has to stand on a platform to play it. The neck is too high for him to reach, and the strings are so thick and heavy anyway, that to press them down you use a series of levers. The lowest note that an octobass can play is actually outside the range of human hearing.

The bigger the better

Making a big instrument isn't always about producing a lower sound. Many guitarists have played instruments with two—or sometimes as many as five—necks. The necks have different arrangements of strings so that the musician can switch, for example, from playing lead guitar to bass guitar without having to swap instruments. In 2011, a guitar museum unveiled the "Rock Ock," which has eight necks, though they can't all be played by a single person.

53. Algaita

The algaita is played in Niger and other parts of West Africa. It is related to the oboe, with a double reed made of wild grass. The two parts of the reed vibrate against each other when the player blows into it. An algaita is made from a hollowed-out piece of wood, with finger holes along its length and a bell at the end.

54. Balaban

The balaban, from Azerbaijan, also has a double reed, but it has a straight body and more finger holes than an algaita. The balaban plays an important part in traditional Azeri music, and archaeologists have found examples of similar instruments from about 2,000 years ago.

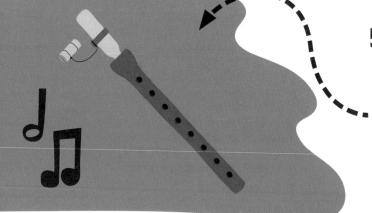

55. Nadaswaram

If you travel to southern India, you might hear a nadaswaram. In fact, the sound of this double-reed instrument is hard to avoid, as it's extremely loud! The long tube of a nadaswaram ends in a wide bell. Nadaswarams are often played at weddings, accompanied by drums.

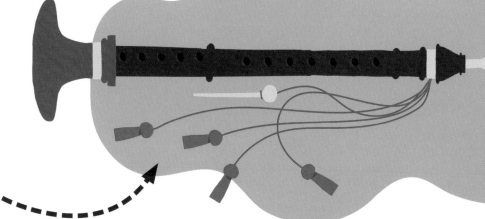

56. Trumpet

The trumpet is one of the best-known brass instruments. It has no reed, so a player vibrates her lips into the mouthpiece, a little like blowing a raspberry. Trumpets are used in a huge range of musical genres: classical, jazz, pop, reggae, mariachi, and more. "Trumpet" is also a general term for any kind of instrument played by vibrating your lips.

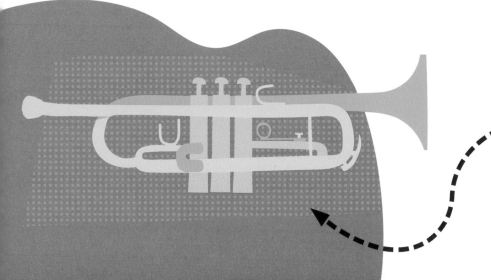

57. Alphorn

The alphorn looks like an overgrown pipe, and it comes—not surprisingly!—from the Alps. Standing on end, these huge trumpets are twice as tall as the people who play them. Their loud sound carries a long way and was perfect for communicating from one village to another in this mountainous region.

58. Serpent

Wouldn't be cool if someone asked you which instrument you play and you could say, "I play the snake"? There really is an old instrument called the serpent, with a body curved like that of a snake. It's a type of trumpet with finger holes along the body. It eventually fell out of fashion and was replaced by the tuba.

59. Didgeridoo

Made from a long, hollow tree branch, didgeridoos are used by the aboriginal people of Australia. Musicians hum and blow into the instrument to create music, and they don't have to stop playing to take a breath. They use a technique called circular breathing—breathing in through the nose at the same time as blowing out from the mouth.

60. Pūtātara

Many cultures around the world have used seashells—especially large conch shells—as natural trumpets to signal over long distances. The pūtātara used by the Maori of New Zealand is one example of this. A carved wooden mouthpiece is tied to the shell using plant fibers.

61. Vuvuzela

If you ever go to a soccer match in South Africa, you'll probably see a vuvuzela. These brightly colored yard-long plastic trumpets are a huge hit with fans, who blow them to cheer on their favorite team.

The original vuvuzelas were made of tin, and many people think they were inspired by the trumpets made from the horn of a kudu (a type of antelope) that once summoned villagers to meetings. Vuvuzelas became world famous thanks to the 2010 FIFA World Cup, which was held in South Africa. Some people compare the sound of a stadium full of vuvuzelas to a swarm of angry bees or a herd of trumpeting elephants.

There are a couple of downsides to the vuvuzela. The first is that most types only play a single pitch, so you can't play a tune on one. The second is that they are really, really loud! Too much time spent in a soccer stadium where vuvuzelas are played can damage your hearing. That's why some shops in South Africa sell earplugs called "Vuvu-Stops"!

62. Saxophone

Antoine-Joseph Sax was so pleased with the instrument he invented that he named it after himself! A saxophone has a single reed that vibrates against a mouthpiece. It is loud, like a brass instrument, but because all ten fingers work the keys to change the pitch, saxophones are better for fast, tricky melodies. Saxophones come in different sizes—the bigger they are, the lower they play. Their mellow sound makes them popular for jazz music.

Woodwind or brass?

In most woodwind instruments, a wooden reed vibrates when the player blows over it. In brass instruments, there is no reed, and the vibrations are created by the player's lips against the mouthpiece.

63. Mijwiz

Like most wind instruments, a clarinet or saxophone can only play one note at a time. The mijwiz, from the Middle East, solves this problem by having two tubes, each with their own reed! The bamboo tubes have finger holes and are tied together, so a player can play both at once. Music played on a mijwiz often accompanies belly dancing.

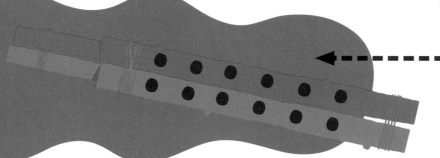

64. Alboka

Played by the Basque people who live along the border between France and Spain, the alboka has two tubes, each with a single reed. The bell is made from a section of cow horn, and another piece of horn covers the reeds. By using circular breathing, an alboka player can produce an uninterrupted sound, like a bagpipe.

65. Kazoo

A toy or a musical instrument? You decide! Invented in the United States in the late 1800s, this simple tube has a thin membrane (similar to the membrane on a dizi) that gives the player's voice a buzzing sound. With most wind instruments, you just blow into them, but a kazoo is different—you have to sing, talk, or hum into it.

66. Sheng

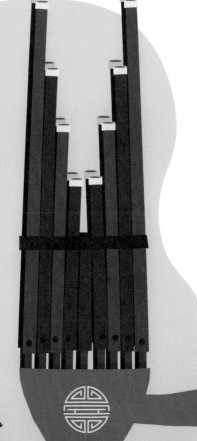

This ancient Chinese instrument has a single mouthpiece connected to a set of tubes—anywhere from 13 to 36 of them! Each tube has a free reed inside, and when a player covers the finger hole on one of the pipes, the reed vibrates to make a sound. The triangular arrangement of the pipes is intended to symbolize the wings of the mythical phoenix.

67. Hulusi

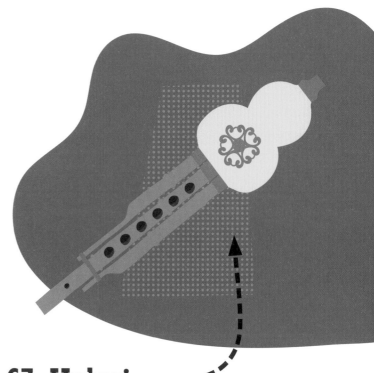

Have you wondered where all the gourds have gone? A few types of wind instruments use them, and the hulusi is one of them. It has three bamboo pipes, each with a free reed, inserted into the bottom of a hollow gourd. A musician blows into a mouthpiece at the top of the gourd and uses finger holes on the bamboo pipes to play a tune. Used in Myanmar and other parts of Southeast Asia, the hulusi sounds a bit like a clarinet.

The amazing human voice

There is one musical instrument that you don't need to make or buy. In fact, it's the oldest instrument there is, and it's found in every corner of the world. Anyone can play it, though the best performers take years of practice to perfect their art. It's the human voice!

How it works

Technically speaking, your voice is a wind instrument. When you speak or sing, your lungs push out air. It travels up your throat and passes through a pair of fleshy flaps (usually called the vocal cords) and makes them vibrate. Hollow spaces in the head and upper body amplify the sound, and other parts of your body—including the tongue, lips, and larynx—modify the buzz of the vocal cords into recognizable speech or music.

Different voices

Vocal cords in men are usually longer and thicker than those in women and children, which is why men usually have deeper voices. In fact, everyone has their own range of notes that they can comfortably produce, and these are grouped into different singing voices. The highest is the soprano, followed by mezzo-soprano and contralto (often called alto). These voices are usually found in women. Then come tenor, baritone, and bass, which are usually sung by men.

Vocal techniques

You might not think that an opera singer and a beatboxer have much in common, but they are both using their voices to create music. They just use different techniques! An opera singer trains their muscles so that they can produce a clear, sustained sound that's powerful enough to be heard at the back of a concert hall. A beatboxer uses their mouth, tongue, and lips to turn their voice into a percussion instrument, creating clicks, rolls, buzzes, drum sounds, and more.

Yodeling is a type of singing that rapidly alternates between high and low notes. It was originally used by shepherds in the Alps to call their animals or to communicate with other villages. Whistling is another vocal technique, which involves puckering the lips and blowing. By changing the shape of the tongue, lips, and throat, a whistler can produce a melody.

Most people can only sing one note at a time, but with the right technique, it's possible to sing two at once! This is called overtone singing or throat singing. Often one note is constant, like a drone, while the singer produces a melody over the top of it. Throat singing is used in folk music by many cultures around the world.

68. Bagpipes

Bagpipes are played in many cultures around the world, but the great Highland bagpipe of Scotland is one of the most famous versions. It is made up of an inflatable bag—traditionally made from an animal skin—with five pipes coming out of it. One is the blowpipe, which you blow into to fill the bag. Three of them are drones with reeds that play a continuous single note. The last pipe, the chanter, has finger holes for playing the melody. Squeezing the bag with your arm keeps air moving through the pipes, even when you've had to stop to take a breath.

69. Accordion

An accordion doesn't look much like a woodwind instrument, does it? You don't have to blow into it, and some versions have a keyboard like a piano! But if you cut an accordion open to look inside, you'd see many reeds, each one covered with a valve. Pressing the keys or buttons on the side of the accordion opens the valve so that air can pass over the reed. The bellows are the central part of the instrument, and squeezing or pulling them forces air over the reeds. The more buttons an accordion has, the more different notes it can play.

MAKE YOUR OWN

To play the flute, you don't blow into it—you blow across an opening in the tube. This makes the air inside the flute vibrate to make a noise. The same thing happens when you blow across the opening at the top of a bottle!

What you need:

- Several narrow-necked bottles (plastic will work, but glass is better, and it's ideal if they're all the same size and shape)
- Water

What to do:

1 Practice blowing across the mouth of one of the bottles to make a note. It may take some experimenting to get the angle right.

2 Now fill the bottle halfway up with water and try again. It should make a higher-pitched sound than before. (This is because there is now less air to vibrate.)

3 Add a different amount of water to each bottle. Play around with adding or removing water until you have a row of bottles that each play a different note.

4 Try to figure out an order of playing the bottles that will produce a song. (Look up videos by a group called the Bottle Boys for inspiration!)

Weird and wonderful instruments

So far, we've traveled the world, looking at instruments that you pluck, bow, scrape, hit, or blow—but the journey isn't over yet. Here are a few of the world's more unusual instruments. Some don't fit neatly into a single category, and as for the others . . . well, they're just plain weird!

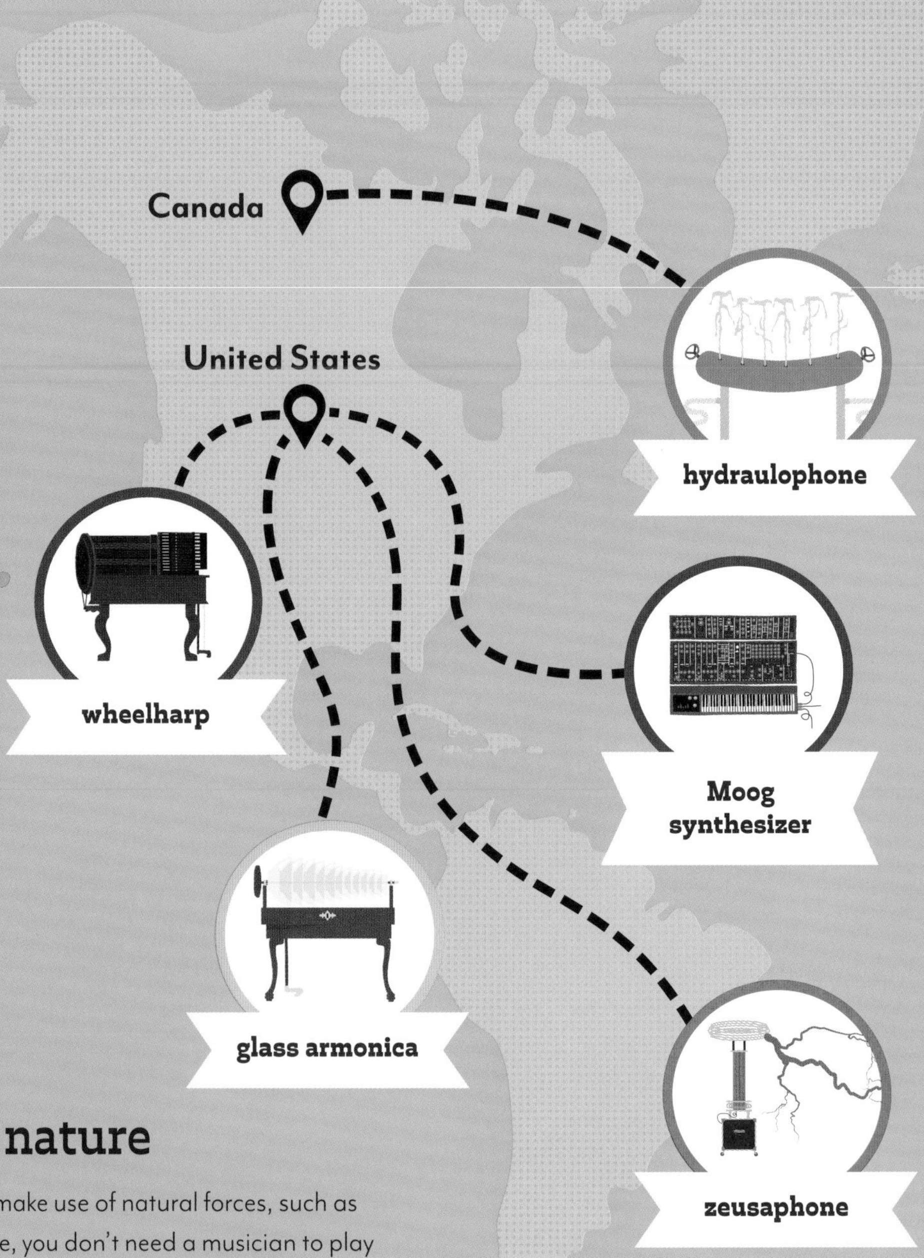

Canada

United States

hydraulophone

wheelharp

Moog synthesizer

glass armonica

zeusaphone

Using nature

You can design instruments that make use of natural forces, such as wind or water. Once they're in place, you don't need a musician to play them! The Singing Ringing Tree, in England, is a hilltop sculpture of metal pipes that sound when the wind blows through or across them. There are similar musical sculptures in many parts of the world.

Just for fun

Some unusual instruments are one of a kind, and they are designed more as works of art than as musical tools. The triolin, which is basically three violins stuck together at the bottom, is a good example of this. Three people have to work together to play it, but it's not easy. Other weird instruments are just for fun. The "loophonium" is a cross between a euphonium and a toilet. It was played as part of a symphony orchestra—but only at their April Fools' concerts!

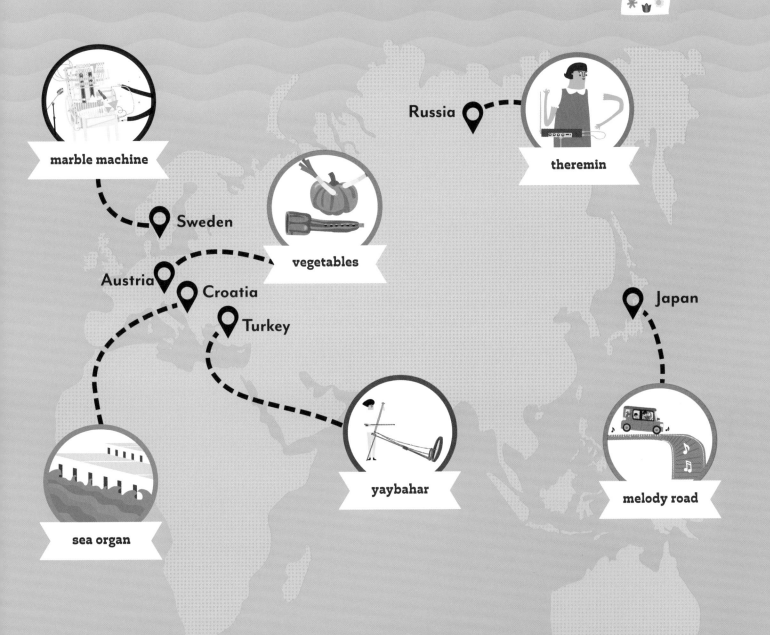

marble machine

Russia

theremin

Sweden

vegetables

Austria

Croatia

Turkey

Japan

sea organ

yaybahar

melody road

That's electric!

In the 20th century, a brand-new family of instruments emerged: ones that use electricity! Electric instruments can do just about anything! There are electric versions of common instruments, but there are others, such as synthesizers, that are completely new types of instruments.

70. Wheelharp

Orchestras usually have large sections of violins, violas, cellos, and double basses. But what if a musician could get the same sound out of a single instrument? With the wheelharp, you can! It's like a hurdy-gurdy on steroids, with a spinning wheel that bows the 61 strings. Each string is played by pressing one of the keys on the piano-style keyboard, and a foot pedal controls the speed of the spinning wheel. With its polished wood and old-style decoration, the wheelharp was designed to look as beautiful as it sounds.

71. Yaybahar

The sounds produced by a yaybahar sound like they come out of a synthesizer, but this instrument doesn't use any electricity. Invented by Turkish musician Görkem Şen, it has two very long coiled springs. One end of each spring is attached to a tall, cello-style neck with two strings. The other end of each spring is attached to a vibrating membrane, like a frame drum. The main way of playing it is by bowing the strings on the neck, which sends vibrations through the springs to the drums to make a range of eerie sounds. You can also hit the membranes with a padded drumstick, or pluck or stroke the springs with your finger.

72. Vegetables

Vegetables are healthy and nutritious —and they can be delicious too. But did you know that they can also be musical? One Austrian band performs entirely on instruments made from vegetables. There are pumpkin drums, hollowed-out radishes made into flutes, peppers turned into trombones, and a carrot xylophone. The "cucumberphone" has a bell pepper bell, a cucumber body, and a carrot mouthpiece. Because vegetables eventually rot, the musicians have to make new instruments for each performance. The scraps are made into soup and served to the audience!

MUSICAL
Road
AHEAD

73. Melody road

Music is everywhere—if you look for it. Have you ever listened to the sound that a car's tires make as it drives along a road? Going over grooves or bumps can change the noise. In Japan there are dozens of "melody roads," where a series of grooves cut into the road plays different notes that you can hear, either inside or outside the car. There's an ulterior motive: the songs only sound right if you're driving at the set speed limit. And a sudden burst of song can make a sleepy driver more alert!

74. Marble machine

Drop a handful of marbles on the floor, and they just make noise. But inside this amazing machine, falling marbles can make beautiful music!

The marble machine, designed by Swedish musician Martin Molin, is a bit like a giant music box. In a normal music box, you use a handle to turn a cylinder that has bumps or pins sticking out of it. When they pass a set of tuned teeth (like the metal strips on an mbira), they play different musical notes.

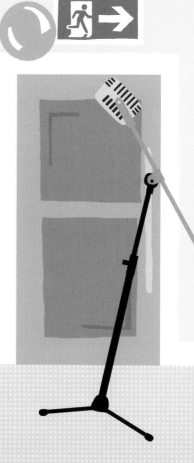

The marble machine, which is cranked by hand, takes the traditional music box design a step further. It has two giant wheels that use LEGO pieces to hit the teeth. Each tooth lifts an arm that releases one of 2,000 marbles. The marble then falls onto one of the different instruments that are part of the machine, including a vibraphone, cymbals, drums, and a bass guitar. As they land, they make a noise. Then they fall into a funnel and are cranked back up to the top, ready to fall again.

Unlike a standard music box, the LEGO pegs on the wheels can be moved around to program a new song. The original marble machine was completed in 2016, and Molin has been busy since then building a new and improved version.

Marvelous mods

Musicians know how to get the best possible sound out of their instruments, but sometimes they want just a little bit more. What if an instrument could play a different range of notes or make a slightly different sound? It's time to break out the modifications!

Music for all

People with disabilities sometimes need instruments that are specially adapted for their needs. For example, there are one-handed versions of the flute, saxophone, and many other instruments. One designer invented a one-handed recorder that can be 3D printed, making it cheap and widely available.

For people with limited finger movement, high-tech gloves can help. You program different hand or finger movements—such as pointing, chopping, or flicking—to match up with a particular instrument sound on a computer. Then you can create music simply by moving your body. It looks a bit like you're playing the air!

The MiMU gloves were the brainchild of Grammy Award–winning recording artist Imogen Heap.

You're too quiet!

In 1899, audio recording was still a new technology, and it worked best with instruments like trumpets, which were loud and projected well. Violins didn't record well at all—that is, until John Stroh invented a new kind of violin. It didn't have a hollow body—just a neck and strings. But they were attached to a metal horn with a vibrating membrane, which amplified the sound. Stroh violins were used for recording for years, and there were also Stroh versions of the viola, cello, and double bass.

Pimp my piano

In a normal piano, the hammers that hit the strings are padded with felt. But if you push thumbtacks or nails into the hammers, they will hit the strings instead, giving a metallic, jangly sound. This is called a tack piano, and it's often heard in Western movies.

Some composers have written music specially for other types of modifed pianos. They place objects on or between the strings to change their sound. They might use anything from screws, coins, and bamboo to erasers, felt, and even forks!

75. Glass armonica

Have you ever made a sound by rubbing your finger along the rim of a glass? The American statesman and thinker Benjamin Franklin invented an instrument that lets you use this technique to play a song. The glass armonica has a lineup of glass bowls, each one tuned to play a different note. The bowls are mounted on an axle that turns when you pump a foot pedal. With your fingers, you can play several glasses at once.

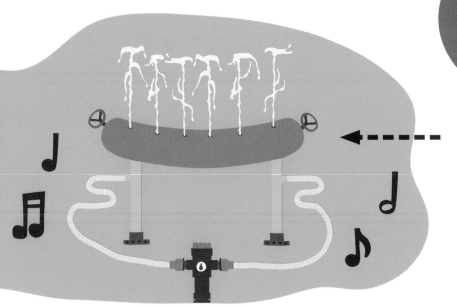

76. Hydraulophone

It's not just blowing wind that can make music— flowing water can do the same when it flows through a hydraulophone. This instrument is a curved tube with finger holes along the top. A pump sends water moving continuously through the tube so it spurts out of the holes. Covering a hole plays a sound, and each hole makes a different pitch. You can cover several holes at once to play a chord!

77. Sea organ

The hydraulophone needs someone to play it, but a sea organ can make music by itself! In the Croatian city of Zadar, concrete steps lead down to the sea. Each one has plastic pipes installed beneath it that have reeds or whistles inside. As waves move across the water and lap up onto the steps, water flows through the pipes to create music that sounds a little like whale song.

78. Theremin

You don't have to blow, hit, or pluck a theremin to make music. In fact, you don't need to touch it at all! Invented in 1920, the theremin was one of the first electronic instruments. It's a box with an antenna on each side. They produce electromagnetic fields, and moving your hands between them disrupts the fields and makes sounds. The theremin's eerie wail is popular in science-fiction movies.

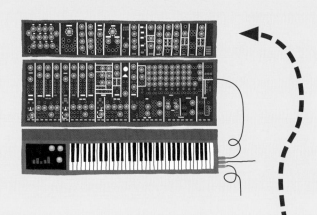

79. Moog synthesizer

Synthesizers can make a huge range of different sounds electronically at the push of a button. They're common today, but when the Moog synthesizer was developed in the 1960s, it was truly groundbreaking. By using keyboards, joysticks, and pedals, a performer could imitate the sounds of strings and horns, as well as produce a range of electronic sounds. It was hugely popular—bands such as the Beatles and the Rolling Stones used it on their albums.

80. Zeusaphone

The zeusaphone is seriously eye-catching—it uses lightning to make music! It's made from a device called a Tesla coil, which produces pulses of electric energy in the form of sparks. The energy heats up the nearby air molecules and makes them vibrate, producing a sound. You can manipulate this to play a tune—accompanied by awesome lightning effects.

The end . . . or the beginning?

So now we've been all around the world, taking in instruments from a range of places and cultures. No matter how different the instruments are, they're all played by people who love music. Are there any that you'd like to pick up and try for yourself? While it might seem as though the journey has ended, it's really only the beginning. The 80 instruments in this book are just a taster. There are hundreds—perhaps thousands—of other instruments to explore!

Over to you

The instruments in this chapter were invented by artists, engineers, and musicians. They came from different backgrounds, but they all had something in common: they wanted to try something new and to make sounds that couldn't be created by the instruments that already existed.

Do you have your own personal vision of a new and exciting sound? If so, then you can try designing your own experimental instrument! It could be a new take on traditional instruments, like the ones that are played by the vegetable orchestra. Or it could be something completely unique, like the theremin—when that was invented, it was like nothing that had come before.

Don't worry, your experimental instrument doesn't have to be as complicated as the marble machine! Look for materials around your home that might be useful, such as rubber bands, plastic bottles, rice or dried beans, balloons, or toilet paper tubes. Can you recycle any unwanted items by turning them into a musical instrument?

Think about what sound you want your instrument to make and how it might work. Will you pluck it, scrape it, shake it, hit it, or blow into it? What parts will it have? How will they work together? Let your imagination run wild!

Index